Gray
Wolves

Other titles in the Returning Wildlife series include:

Returning Wildlife

Gray Wolves

John E. Becker

KIDHAVEN
PRESS™

THOMSON

GALE

San Diego • Detroit • New York • San Francisco • Cleveland
New Haven, Conn. • Waterville, Maine • London • Munich

LIBRARY OF CONGRESS CATALOGING-IN-PUBLICATION DATA

Becker, John E., 1942–
  Gray wolves / by John E. Becker.
    v. cm. — (Returning wildlife)
Summary: Describes the physical characteristics, behavior, and history of
endangered wolves and attempts being made to ensure their survival.
Includes bibliographical references and index.
  ISBN 0-7377-1378-X (hardback : alk. paper)
  1. Wolves—Juvenile literature. [1. Wolves. 2. Endangered species. 3. Wildlife
conservation.] I. Title. II. Series.
  QL737.C22B398 2004
  599.773—dc21

2003003942

Contents

chapter 1

Gray Ghosts

Gray wolves lived in North America for thousands of years before European settlers arrived in the sixteenth century. The settlers considered wolves a threat to themselves and their livestock. They used guns, poisons, and traps to kill wolves wherever they found them. Early in the twentieth century, the U.S. government joined the war on wolves by introducing predator control programs that were aimed at destroying the animals. By 1970 gray wolves had been eliminated from all of their former range in the lower forty-eight states, except for a few hundred that survived in the western Great Lakes region.

When gray wolves were given protection by the Endangered Species Act in the 1970s, they began to recover. By 2002 there were more than four thousand gray wolves once again living in the lower forty-eight states.

Wolves Through the Ages

Approximately 35 million years ago, doglike mammals with long legs for running fast first appeared on Earth. Those animals gave rise to modern wolves about 1 million years ago. Wolves developed into excellent predators and crossed the land bridge between Asia and North America during several **ice ages** in search of prey animals. Thereafter, wolves lived throughout the Northern Hemisphere. Three types of wolves—red wolves, gray wolves, and dire wolves (which became extinct seventeen thousand years ago)—lived in North America.

Today, red wolves and gray wolves survive in greatly reduced numbers in the United States. During the twentieth century, red wolves disappeared in the wild, but were preserved in captivity. People have **reintroduced** red wolves into parts of North Carolina as a first step in reestablishing the red wolf population in the American Southeast.

Wolf Anatomy

Long skull supports a large brain and acts as an anchor for powerful jaw muscles.

Large canine teeth for catching and holding prey.

Streamlined body and camouflage fur coat.

Long slender limbs for running up to 45 mph.

Large flexible feet and sharp claws for gripping and climbing.

Large pointed ears and long, sensitive nose for tracking prey.

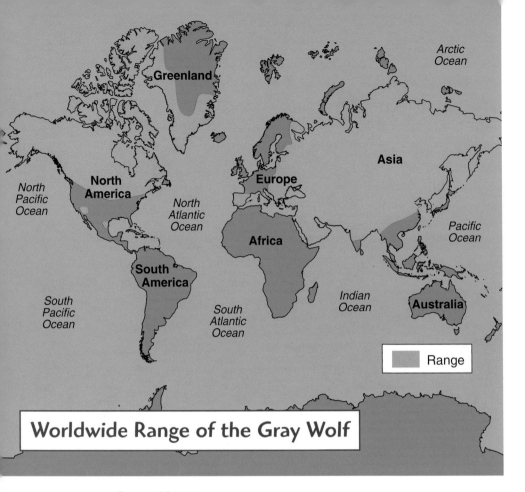

Worldwide Range of the Gray Wolf

Map labels: Greenland, North America, North Pacific Ocean, North Atlantic Ocean, South America, South Pacific Ocean, South Atlantic Ocean, Europe, Africa, Asia, Arctic Ocean, Pacific Ocean, Indian Ocean, Australia, Range

Gray Wolves

Gray wolves are the largest members of the **canid**, or dog, family. A large male gray wolf may be up to six feet in length from its nose to the tip of its tail, stand almost three feet tall at the shoulder, and weigh more than 130 pounds. A small female gray wolf, on the other hand, may weigh as little as sixty pounds. Usually, female gray wolves are smaller and lighter than males.

Gray wolves may be white, black, or any combination of those colors plus tan, rust, brown, or gold. A variety of colors may be represented within the same litter of pups.

Today, gray wolves are found only in a few areas of the United States. They live in Alaska; in the western Great Lakes region of Minnesota, Wisconsin, and Michigan; in the Rocky Mountain region of Idaho, Montana, and Wyoming; and in the southwest region of Arizona and New Mexico.

Before the arrival of European settlers, gray wolves' geographic range extended from the Atlantic coast to the Pacific coast and from Canada to Mexico. Gray wolves were able to successfully inhabit most of North America in large part because they lived and hunted together.

A Big Paw!

● How big is your hand compared to this life-size gray wolf paw print?

The Wolf Pack

Wolves live in family groups called packs. A pack is usually made up of related wolves. These include an **alpha pair**, their offspring, and other adult wolves. The alpha pair leads the pack, and they are the wolves that breed. In general, the alpha pair will not permit other wolves in the pack to breed. Usually, superior strength, intelligence, hunting ability, and other leadership skills allow the alpha pair to be **dominant** over the other wolves in the pack.

A wolf pack generally lives in and defends a certain territory. This territory can range from fifty square miles to as much as one thousand square miles. Packs constantly check for signs of other wolves trespassing in their territory. A strange wolf discovered within the pack's territory will usually be driven off or killed.

Wolves communicate to other wolves in the pack in a number of ways. Scientists believe that wolves use howls to identify each other, to call the pack together, or to warn other wolves to stay out of their territory. Wolves use other sounds such as whines to show affection, growls to show anger, and barking to sound an alarm.

Wolves also communicate through body language. A wolf standing tall with its head, ears, and tail up is communicating dominance or confidence. A wolf whose head, ears, and tail are down, on the other hand, is a **submissive** or fearful wolf.

Natural Predators

Wolves are very good hunters. They have a number of characteristics that allow them to locate and kill prey. For example, wolves are very intelligent. A wolf's brain is larger than the brain of a dog of the same size. Wolves also have sharp teeth and extremely powerful jaws. The

A wolf pack howls in the snow. Howling is a form of wolf communication.

crushing bite of a wolf is significantly stronger than that of a German shepherd. Wolves have an extremely well developed sense of smell. Scientists believe that a wolf's sense of smell may be one hundred times greater than that of a human. In addition, wolves can hear very well. They have the ability to hear sounds that people cannot hear.

Wolves can also run very fast and very far. Wolves can run as fast as forty-five miles per hour. This allows them to capture quick-moving prey. They can also run at slower speeds for great distances. Wolves have been known to travel more than thirty miles in one day.

Because they hunt together, wolves are able to kill large animals such as deer, moose, elk, and bison. Wolves

Wolves feast on a young moose they killed. Wolves hunt together to kill animals as big as moose.

also eat smaller animals, including beaver, squirrels, rabbits, and mice. However, they need large prey to survive from year to year. Wolves eat up to twenty pounds of meat at one time (this is comparable to a person eating eighty quarter-pound hamburgers at one meal).

Raising a Family

Wolves are able to breed by the time they are twenty-two months old. The breeding season for gray wolves is January through March. Pups are usually born in April or May, and litters include four to eight pups. Pups weigh about one pound, are blind, and are completely helpless at birth.

Female wolves give birth in a den. Dens can be in a riverbank, a hollow log, a cave, an abandoned fox den, or under tree roots. Mothers and their newborn pups occupy the den, while other wolves stand guard outside.

    The birth of pups is a time of great excitement for a wolf pack. The wolf mother nurses the pups for the first five weeks of life, while other members of the pack bring her food. When the pups are two weeks old, their

A gray wolf cub howls for the first time. Pups grow very quickly.

eyes open, and a week later they can hear. By four weeks old, the pups leave the den to explore the outside world.

Wolf pups grow quickly. They are almost the size of an adult wolf by six months of age. A pup will stay with the pack for the first year of its life. After one year, pups either move on or become full-time members of the pack. Young wolves that move on search for a mate so they can start a pack of their own. These "lone wolves" try to avoid other packs because they may be killed for encroaching on another pack's territory.

Less than half of all wolf pups live to become adults. But those that do will live from six to ten years of age in the wild.

Wide Range of Habitats

Wolves are very adaptable animals. They seem to be equally at home in deserts, arctic plains, forests, or prairies. Wherever there are prey animals, wolves can be found. Despite their ability to adapt, however, wolves have suffered from the loss of wilderness areas and from being killed by people.

chapter 2

War on Wolves

Each year wolves die from natural causes. Some get diseases. Others die in fights with mountain lions, bison, elk, or other wolves. These natural causes helped to keep wolf populations in balance for centuries. But when Europeans arrived in North America they declared war on wolves, and the wolf populations declined to dangerously low levels.

The Wolf Threat

Europeans believed that wolves were evil, bloodthirsty creatures. Stories of wolves attacking people and their livestock were common in European countries. Therefore, the early European settlers in North America were convinced that the wolves in this new land were also a threat to themselves and their animals. It did not take long before the settlers' fears for their livestock were realized.

While clearing land, establishing farms, and building settlements, the Europeans killed deer, elk, bison, and other animals that were the prey of wolves. Without their natural prey, the wolves turned to the settlers' cows, sheep, goats, pigs, and chickens to survive. To protect their livestock, settlers used every method available to kill wolves. Wolves were shot and trapped. And when the settlers discovered that wolves return to a partially eaten kill, they used poison to kill the wolves. Poisoning the remains of partially eaten kills was so effective that it became the preferred way to "deal with the wolf problem."

Sheep are a favorite meal for wolves when their natural prey is in short supply.

Bounties on Wolves

As early as 1630, just ten years after the Pilgrims landed in America, the Massachusetts Bay Colony passed laws encouraging people to kill wolves. The killing of a wolf was considered an important public service because wolves were seen as a threat to the Pilgrims' survival. A person who killed a wolf was given a reward called a bounty. The bounty for killing a wolf was equal to a month's wages, so colonists were eager to hunt down as many wolves as they could.

Paying bounties for killing wolves quickly spread to other colonies. The Virginia Bay Colony began offering a bounty on wolves in 1632. South Carolina did the same in 1695. And by 1697 New Jersey also offered bounties for dead wolves.

As pioneers pushed westward from the Atlantic coast, they cleared the land and collected bounties for killing wolves wherever they settled. Bounties on wolves were offered for the first time in Pennsylvania in 1705. Then in 1818 pioneers in Hinckley, Ohio, organized a hunt to rid the area of bears and wolves. More than six hundred people participated in the "Great Hinckley Hunt," which offered bounties of fifteen dollars each for wolf scalps. Seventeen wolves, twenty-one bears, and numerous other animals were killed during the hunt.

By the 1850s, pioneers were settling the middle of the country, and they continued killing wolves as they moved into each new territory. Shortly after Iowa became a state in 1856, the state senate considered a law to protect the sheep industry in Iowa by paying a three-dollar bounty for each dead wolf.

This wolf caught his foot in a hunter's trap. American pioneers hunted wolves in the areas they settled.

Wolves Slowly Disappear

After the Civil War ended in 1865, Americans continued waging war on wolves. Americans also killed many of the wolves' prey animals. The primary prey of wolves on the Great Plains, the American bison, became the object of intensive hunting during the last decades of the nineteenth century. At first, bison were killed for their meat

Men shoot bison from a train. Such mass killing made it difficult for wolves to find food.

and skins. Later, they were hunted almost to extinction as part of a government strategy to defeat the Plains Indian tribes and force them onto reservations. More than 30 million bison disappeared, as did other prey animals that wolves depended on for survival.

The territory that had been home to huge bison herds was turned into farms. Thus, out of necessity, wolves began to kill the farmers' livestock for food. Plans were soon developed to wipe out wolves, and hunters, known as wolfers, were eager to do their part.

Wolf Hunters

From the mid-1800s until the 1880s, the price of wolf pelts steadily increased. During that time, many wolfers made a living hunting wolves. Between 1870 and 1877, hundreds of wolves were killed each year in Montana alone. A farmworker during that period earned about fifty cents per day. A hunter was paid $1.25 per pelt; therefore, a skilled wolfer could make much more money killing wolves.

As campaigns to destroy wolves became common in America, wolves began disappearing from one section of the country after another. The last known wolf to be killed in the Northeast died in 1897. By 1900 gray wolves had disappeared from almost all of the eastern United States. Only a few hundred remained in the western Great Lakes area.

Even this was not enough to satisfy the federal government, though. In 1907 rangers in national parks were ordered to hunt down and kill wolves they encountered there. In addition, livestock organizations funded by wealthy ranchers in western states offered extremely high bounties in an effort to destroy the remaining wolves in that part of the country. In 1909 the Club Ranch in Colorado offered a $50 bounty per wolf. A few years later the Piceance Creek Stock Growers Association in Colorado offered $150 bounties on wolves. At a time when the average weekly salary for an American worker was less than $20, some bounty hunters earned as much as $1,000 per week hunting wolves.

Predator Control Programs

In 1915 the U.S. government increased its efforts to destroy wolves when Congress approved funding for a predator control program known as Animal Damage Control (ADC). ADC's goal was to eliminate destructive animals such as wolves, grizzly bears, mountain lions, and coyotes from the United States. The U.S. Biological Survey (USBS) was the government agency put in charge of administering the program. The USBS hired bounty

Arctic wolf skins hang on a fur trader's line. Wolf pelts were very valuable.

Ted Turner, owner of the Atlanta Braves, and biologists release a wolf on his ranch in New Mexico. Scientists are working to return wolves to the wild.

hunters and sent them out to kill any wolves they could find.

The program was successful. By 1926 gray wolves no longer roamed the Great Plains. In 1940 the last wolf was killed in the state of Washington. A few wolves managed to survive in remote areas of northern Minnesota and the southwestern United States near the Mexican border in Texas and Arizona. But gray wolves had been eliminated from every other part of the country. Then in 1970 the last Mexican wolves in the United States disappeared, and the population in Mexico was reduced to a handful of animals. From the beginning of the ADC program until 1970, USBS hunters killed approximately seventy thousand wolves.

Few Wolves Survive

By the 1970s, only a few hundred gray wolves survived in the lower forty-eight states. Attitudes toward wildlife in general, and wolves in particular, were changing, however, and many people across the country were determined to restore America's wolf population.

chapter 3

A Long Road Back

A loud whirring sound in the sky caused the wolf pack to break into a run. Before the wolves could get up to full speed, a bright red and white helicopter hovered directly above them. A man in the helicopter aimed his rifle at one of the wolves and then slowly pulled the trigger. He made a direct hit in the rear of the wolf. The wolf stumbled slightly from the impact but continued running. Before long the wolf began to slow down. Then it collapsed in the snow.

The helicopter landed nearby. Two scientists jumped out and ran over to the sleeping wolf. They quickly removed the **tranquilizer** dart and began giving the wolf a physical examination.

Once the scientists were sure that the wolf was healthy, they attached a lightweight radio collar that will allow them to follow the movements of the wolf for the next several months. By studying this wolf and many others, scientists will learn important information that will make it possible to return wolves to wilderness areas across the United States.

Wolf Recovery

After many years of destroying wolves, the federal government took a major step toward restoring them in 1973 when Congress passed the Endangered Species Act (ESA). Gray wolves were one of the species listed as endangered under the ESA. The law requires that each endangered species be restored to healthy population

A biologist removes a radio collar from a tranquilized wolf. Scientists use radio collars to study wolves in the wild.

levels and that habitat also be restored to ensure the survival of the species in the future. Gray wolf recovery in the United States has focused on three geographic regions: the western Great Lakes, northern Rocky Mountains, and the Southwest.

24

Western Great Lakes Wolves

At the time the ESA became law, there were approximately one thousand wolves living in the western Great Lakes region of the United States. This area includes the states of Minnesota, Wisconsin, and Michigan. A recovery plan for wolves in the western Great Lakes was approved in 1978.

Once they were given protection and their main prey, white-tailed deer, were restored, gray wolves rapidly increased in numbers and spread out into new territory. Since the 1970s, the range for wolves in the state of Minnesota has increased to include most of the northern counties in the state. The goal of having twelve to fourteen hundred wolves living in Minnesota was reached by 1978. In 2002 the population was estimated at twenty-six hundred.

As the wolf population in Minnesota increased, wolves began to migrate, or move, from Minnesota into northern Wisconsin. Wolves had disappeared from Wisconsin by 1960. But once they were given legal protection, they quickly moved back into the good habitat that existed in the northern parts of the state. These areas had plenty of prey animals and few people. By 2002 the gray wolf population in Wisconsin was estimated to be 250.

Few wolves survived in the state of Michigan after the 1950s. But in the late 1980s wolf sightings became more frequent in Michigan's Upper Peninsula, located next to northern Wisconsin. Wolves from Minnesota, Wisconsin, and Ontario, Canada, have now repopulated the entire Upper Peninsula of Michigan. In 2002 the wolf population in Michigan was approximately 280.

Gray wolf population growth has exceeded the goals set by the Western Great Lakes Recovery Plan. As a result, the U.S. Fish and Wildlife Service, the governmental agency in charge of restoring endangered species, is considering recommending that the wolves of the western Great Lakes region be removed from the endangered species list.

A gray wolf enjoys a meal of fresh deer. The gray wolf population is slowly recovering.

A gray wolf pup runs through a river in Montana. Wolves have been reintroduced in Montana with some success.

Northern Rocky Mountains

By the 1920s, wolves had disappeared from the northern Rocky Mountain region of the United States. This area includes the states of Wyoming, Montana, and Idaho. In 1974 the Fish and Wildlife Service appointed a northern Rocky Mountain wolf recovery team to develop a plan for returning wolves to the northern Rocky Mountains.

The plan was completed in 1980. It set a goal of reestablishing healthy wolf populations in northwestern Wyoming, western Montana, and central Idaho. Experts felt that these three areas had good wolf habitat, large numbers of prey animals, and few domestic livestock, an ideal situation for returning wolves. In 1982 a wolf pack migrated into Glacier National Park in northern Montana from Canada. Four years later the first litter of wolf pups in fifty years was born in the park.

Then in 1991, the government decided to reintroduce wolves to other parts of the Rocky Mountain region. In January 1995, fifteen wolves were captured in Canada and released in central Idaho. In March of that same year fourteen wolves were captured in Canada and released in Yellowstone National Park, located in Montana, Wyoming, and Idaho. Wolves were also released in 1996. Reintroduced wolves in Yellowstone and Idaho have had many pups and few conflicts with humans. They have also survived at a higher rate than predicted. In 2002 there were between 650 and 700 wolves in the northern Rocky Mountain area.

Mexican Wolves

The Mexican wolf, also known as lobo (Spanish for "wolf"), is the smallest subspecies of gray wolf in North America. For thousands of years, lobos roamed the woodlands, grasslands, and cactus-studded landscape of Texas, New Mexico, Arizona, and Mexico. In 1976, when scientists expressed their concern that lobos could no longer be found in the United States, they were added to the endangered species list. A Mexican wolf recovery team was assembled in 1979 to develop strategies for the recovery of lobos.

In 1980 the last lobo was shot in the wild in Mexico. Fortunately, five lobos had been captured in Mexico between 1977 and 1980. They formed the founding stock for a **captive-breeding** program to ensure the survival of the Mexican wolf. Captive breeding, breeding animals held in zoos and other facilities, was the main strategy employed to help lobos recover. The lobos bred quite well in captivity, and soon several captive-breeding facilities were raising lobo pups. By 1982 scientists had prepared a plan to return the captive-born lobos to the wild in the American Southwest.

It was sixteen years before the scientists were ready to put their plan into action. But finally, in 1998, the first eleven captive-bred lobos were released into the wild in Arizona. This attempt did not go well. A year after their release, only two of the lobos were still in the wild. The others had been shot, hit by a car, had disappeared, or were returned to captivity. Despite the setback, the release program continued. Between 1998 and 2002, another sixty-three wolves were released in Arizona and New Mexico.

By 2002 there were more than two hundred lobos being held in forty-three captive facilities. There were also seven known packs of lobos located in Arizona and New Mexico that have produced litters of pups in the wild. At least forty lobos now roam the American Southwest, and they are expanding their territory each year.

This Mexican wolf was bred in captivity and released into the wild.

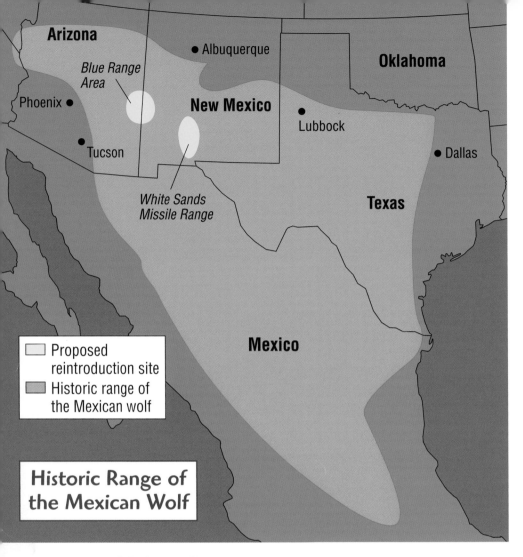

Arizona

Blue Range
Area

Phoenix •

Tucson •

• Albuquerque

New Mexico

Oklahoma

Lubbock •

Dallas •

White Sands
Missile Range

Texas

Mexico

☐ Proposed
reintroduction site
▨ Historic range of
the Mexican wolf

**Historic Range of
the Mexican Wolf**

Making Progress

Recovery programs have experienced setbacks from
time to time. But gray wolves have recovered so successfully in the western Great Lakes and the northern
Rocky Mountains that the government has recom-
mended that their protected status be reduced from
endangered to threatened. A number of conservation
organizations are opposed to the plan, however. They
fear that lessening protection may lead to gray wolves
disappearing once again. The debate over the status of
gray wolves will undoubtedly continue into the fore-
seeable future.

chapter 4

A Promising Future

A licia Shelley, a zookeeper at Ohio's Columbus Zoo, approached the window of the Mexican wolf exhibit. When the wolves saw her, they trotted back and forth along the back of the exhibit.

After looking at the wolves to make sure that they all appeared healthy, Alicia turned to a television mounted above the glass. The television showed the wolves' pups in their den. Being able to observe the pups lets zookeepers check on the five young wolves without disturbing them, or their mother. The television also allows zoo visitors to see the pups.

Once she was satisfied that the wolf pups were active and in good health, Alicia spoke to three high school students who had been observing the wolves. The students were gaining valuable experience for a class in wildlife management offered jointly by the zoo and local high schools.

The Columbus Zoo is just one of more than forty facilities in the United States and Mexico keeping Mexican wolves. Since 1992 the Columbus Zoo has raised sixteen Mexican wolf pups. And in 2000 a male Mexican wolf from the zoo was released in Arizona.

Problems for Wolves

Even though wolves have made a comeback in the American wilderness, there are still many things that threaten their survival. Humans remain the biggest problem. Many people still believe that wolves are a

Zookeeper Alicia Shelley works with wolves at the Columbus Zoo.

threat to them. That feeling persists despite the fact that no one has ever died from a wild wolf attack in North America.

Many farmers and ranchers also still believe that wolves are a threat to their livestock. Scientists who study wolves, however, claim that if plenty of natural prey such as white-tailed deer is available, wolves are less likely to attack livestock. In many cases, simply using protective measures for livestock, such as building fences or using trained guard dogs, can keep wolves from killing livestock. Unfortunately, some livestock owners take the law into their own hands and illegally kill wolves on or near their property.

This illegal killing, or poaching, of wolves continues to be a serious concern. Some people still shoot, poison, or trap wolves to protect their animals, even in areas where wolves have not killed livestock. The poaching of wolves could threaten the survival of the species. Because of this threat, anyone killing a wolf illegally faces a fine of up to $100,000 and/or one year in jail.

Wolves in the Northeast

In addition to the problem of poaching, America's wilderness areas disappear at an alarming rate each year. Reintroducing wolves and giving them legal protection will

A loan wolf stops traffic. Humans continue to invade wolf habitat.

not ensure their survival if there are no wild places for them to live. The future is not entirely bleak, however. More reintroduction projects are under consideration for the parts of the country where good wolf habitat remains.

Some experts believe that the Northeast contains some of the best wolf habitat in America. In fact, a 26-million-acre corridor of good wolf habitat extends from the Adirondack Mountains in New York through Maine. Wolves were eliminated from that part of the country in the late nineteenth century. But now plans are being developed to bring wolves back to the Northeast. A plan known as the Eastern Timber Wolf Recovery Plan has identified areas in Maine, northern New Hampshire, and northern New York as possible sites for gray wolf reintroductions.

Unfortunately, many state legislators in those areas are opposed to wolf reintroductions because of pressure from hunting groups that fear that wolves will prey on game animals such as white-tailed deer. The New Hampshire legislature, for example, has passed a measure that would prevent wolves from being reintroduced to that state. The issue is still being debated in New York, Maine, and Vermont, and the controversy will undoubtedly continue well into the future. Occasional wolf sightings in the Northeast, however, suggest that even as people argue about wolves, the animals may already be moving into the region from Canada.

The Southern Rocky Mountains

Fortunately, there are many other places in the country that have good wolf habitat, and lawmakers in some of these areas are more open to wolf reintroductions. Some of the last places wolves disappeared from were the rugged mountains of Colorado, Wyoming, and New

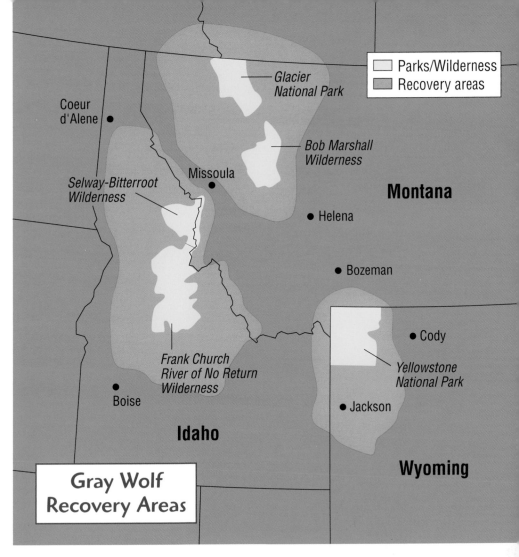

Parks/Wilderness
Recovery areas

Glacier
National Park

Coeur
d'Alene

Bob Marshall
Wilderness

Selway-Bitterroot
Wilderness

Missoula

Montana

Helena

Bozeman

Cody

Frank Church
River of No Return
Wilderness

Yellowstone
National Park

Boise

Jackson

Idaho

Wyoming

**Gray Wolf
Recovery Areas**

Mexico. Scientists believe that ideal wolf habitat exists in the Rocky Mountains, which stretch from southern Wyoming to northern New Mexico. This area has both healthy populations of prey animals that gray wolves need for survival and relatively few people.

Adding this vast region to the existing gray wolf recovery zones would help link wolf populations in the southern Rockies with those in Montana, Idaho, and Canada. This would reestablish a route allowing the free movement of wolves from Mexico to Canada. A scientific study in 1994 indicated that the Colorado portion of this region could support more than one thousand wolves.

There also seems to be strong public support for the wolf reintroduction plan in that area.

The Pacific Northwest

Yet another possible site for restoring gray wolves is the Pacific Northwest. Wolves from Idaho have already migrated into parts of eastern Oregon and Washington, and scientists believe that more wolves will follow. Wolf migration from Canada into the north Cascade Mountains and Selkirk Mountains of northern Washington is also expected.

Scientists also believe that good wolf habitat and healthy numbers of prey animals exist in northern Cali-

A rancher tends to a sheep. Some ranchers believe that wolves released in the wild threaten their sheep.

fornia. Areas of northern California, therefore, appear to be well suited for gray wolf recovery. Livestock owners in the area are generally opposed to wolf recovery, but other people who live in that region are in favor of restoring wolves.

Helping Wolves Recover

People are helping to set the stage for wolves to return to their former habitat in many ways. One way that people have helped wolves has been by creating protected areas across the United States where wolves can be reintroduced. The establishment of national parks, wildlife refuges, national forests, and wilderness areas has added huge tracts of protected habitat where wolves have been returned. Hopefully, the trend toward adding more protected areas will continue into the future.

Yet another way that people are making it easier for wolves to recover is by providing predator compensation programs, which give payments to farmers and ranchers who lose livestock to wolves. These programs are an important part of any successful reintroduction program for predators. In the western Great Lakes region, losses are paid for by the states. But in the rest of the country, payments are made by the Bailey Wildlife Foundation Wolf Compensation Trust. If an animal owned by a farmer or rancher is killed by a wolf, the Bailey trust pays the owner a fair price to replace the dead animal. Knowing that they will not be losing money because of wolves has changed the attitude of some farmers and ranchers who had opposed wolf reintroductions.

Educating the Public

Many private conservation organizations are also helping to educate children and adults about the need to preserve wolves. At Wolf Park, a private education and research

An animal handler at Indiana's Wolf Park talks to one of the wolves. The park educates the public about wolves.

facility located in Indiana, children not only learn about wolves but can become junior volunteers. The volunteer program accepts children ages seven through seventeen who are interested in learning about animal care and animal behavior. A junior volunteer at Wolf Park may help with park maintenance, work in the office, or work directly with park visitors. Volunteers also learn skills that may form the basis for an animal-related career such as veterinary science.

The International Wolf Center in Ely, Minnesota, is another important source of information about wolves.

Located in the heart of Minnesota's wolf country, the center has educated visitors and people around the world about wolves and the urgent need for a greater understanding of these animals. Taking accurate information about wolves into schools and other locations is the focus of the center's mission.

A Hopeful Outlook

With gray wolves successfully returning to the western Great Lakes, the Southwest, and the northern Rocky Mountains, the future for wolves in the United States appears promising. Wolf recovery, however, is not assured because many people continue to oppose wolf restoration. At least now wolves have a fighting chance to survive.

alpha pair: The male and female pair of wolves that control all the other wolves in a pack.

canid: A member of the dog family Canidae, which includes domestic dogs, wolves, jackals, and coyotes.

captive breeding: The breeding of animals held in captive facilities such as zoos.

dominant: The highest-ranking member of a group that controls the other members of the group.

ice age: A geological era when much of the Northern Hemisphere was covered in great ice sheets.

reintroduce: To introduce again, as in returning animals to areas from which they disappeared.

submissive: To be weak or under the control of another.

tranquilizer: A drug that causes drowsiness and sleep.

Books

Karen Dudley, *The Untamed World: Wolves*. Austin, TX: Raintree Steck-Vaughn, 1997. Discusses the physical characteristics and behaviors of wolves, their social organization, and the myths and legends surrounding wolves.

Barbara Keevil Parker, *North American Wolves*. Minneapolis, MN: Carolrhoda Books, 1998. Describes the physical characteristics, behaviors, and struggle for survival of gray wolves and red wolves in North America.

Dorothy Hinshaw Patent, *Gray Wolf, Red Wolf*. New York: Clarion Books, 1990. Explains the characteristics of the two species of wolves native to North America and looks at efforts to restore wolves to their natural habitat in America.

Stephen R. Swinburne, *Once a Wolf*. Boston: Houghton Mifflin, 1999. Examines the turbulent relationship between people and wolves, the changing view of the importance of predators to a balanced environment, and the reintroduction of wolves to the Yellowstone ecosystem.

Periodicals

Gary Ferguson, "Living the Wild Life," *Boys' Life*, December 2001. Follows wildlife biologist Dr. Doug Smith as he tranquilizes a wolf in Yellowstone National Park and explains the urgent need to restore wolves to their natural environment across the United States.

Barbara Keevil Parker, "Wolf Talk," *Boys' Quest*, October/November 1997. Describes the various ways in which wolves communicate, including howls, body language, and facial expressions.

Organizations to Contact

Defenders of Wildlife

National Headquarters
1101 14th Street NW #1400
Washington, DC 20005
(202) 682-9400
www.defenders.org

An organization dedicated to the conservation of all native wild animals and plants.

International Wolf Center

1396 Highway 169
Ely, MN 55731-8129
(218) 365-4695
www.wolf.org

An organization dedicated to educating people around the world about wolves and their conservation.

The Wild Canid Center

P.O. Box 760
Eureka, MO 63025
(636) 938-5900
www.wolfsanctuary.org

This organization is concerned with the successful captive breeding of red wolves, Mexican wolves, and maned wolves and restoring them to their natural habitat.

Wolf Haven International

3111 Offut Lake Road
Tenino, WA 98589
(360) 264-4695
www.wolfhaven.org

This organization promotes wolf conservation, reestablishing wolves in their historic range, and public education about the value of all wildlife.

Wolf Park
Battle Ground, IN 47920
(765) 567-2265
www.wolfpark.org

An education and research organization devoted to the study of wolf behavior.

Video

Wolves: A Legend Returns to Yellowstone. National Geographic, 2000. Details the struggle for survival of a wolf pack after wolves were reintroduced into Yellowstone National Park.

Dr. John E. Becker writes books and magazine articles about nature and wild animals for children. He graduated from Ohio State University in the field of education. He has been an elementary school teacher, college professor, and zoo administrator. Dr. Becker has also worked in the field of wildlife conservation with the International Society of Endangered Cats. He currently lives in Delaware, Ohio, and teaches writing at the Thurber Writing Academy. He also enjoys visiting schools and sharing his love of writing with kids. In his spare time, Dr. Becker likes to read, hike in the woods, ice skate, and play tennis.